## My background

Name: ______________________________

School: ______________________________

Favourite places: ______________________________

______________________________

______________________________

Favourite animals: ______________________________

______________________________

______________________________

# Before you begin writing ...

## Posture

1. Sit up straight at your table.
2. Put your feet flat on the floor.
3. Keep your wrist straight and resting on the table.

## Pen grip

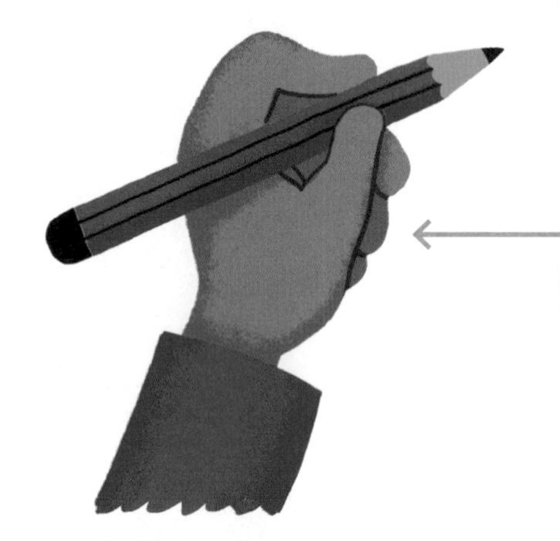

Left-handed

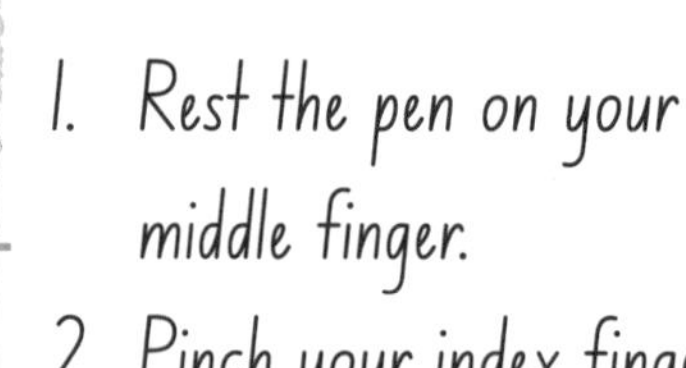

1. Rest the pen on your middle finger.
2. Pinch your index finger and thumb together gently.

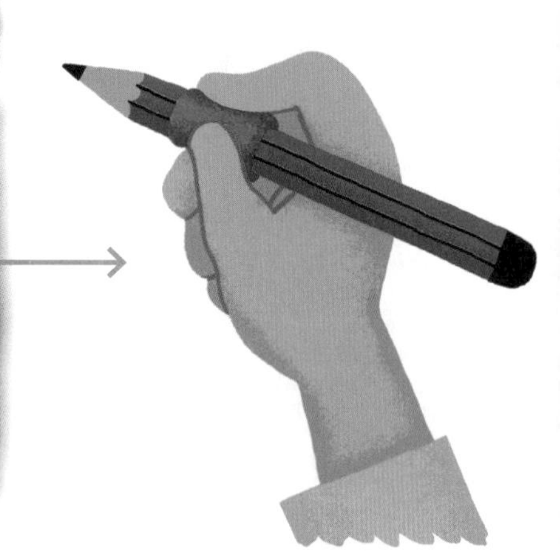

Right-handed

## Paper

Left-handed

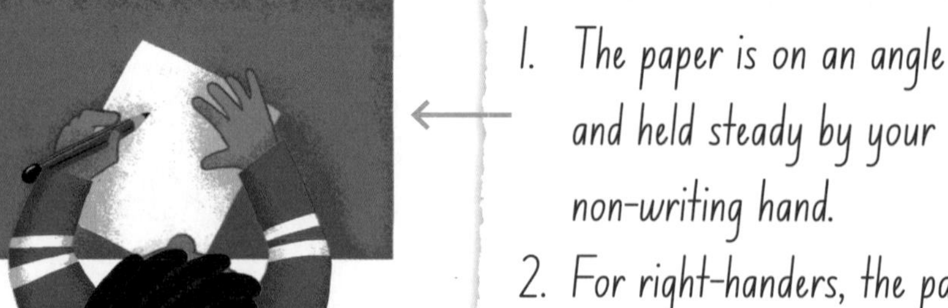

1. The paper is on an angle and held steady by your non-writing hand.
2. For right-handers, the page will tilt to the left.
3. For left-handers, the page will tilt to the right.

Right-handed

# Revision

## Letter formation

Before we start, let's revise the different types of handwriting. Remember that cursive handwriting is best for everyday writing and print handwriting is ideal for labelling maps and diagrams.

Practise writing the letters below. Then colour in the landscape.

A a B b C c D d E e F f G g H h I i

J j K k L l M m N n O o P p Q q R r

S s T t U u V v W w X x Y y Z z

In cursive handwriting, write your first and last name.

In cursive handwriting, write today's date.

Copy these punctuation marks:

. , " " ' ? ! ; :

In your neatest handwriting, copy the sentence below.

Excellent handwriting is easy to read.

# Diagonal joins

Before you begin, complete the checklist below.

- ☐ I have my feet flat on the floor.
- ☐ My back is up nice and straight.
- ☐ I can hold my pen accurately.

diagonal join

in

Practise your diagonal joins as you copy the letters, words and sentences below.

le ne in am du de ur er zi ly un ci

uc he ty is ky mi ui ti te li an ce

sustain life planet living ecosystem connected

intricate world animals plants organisms physical

food components system supports wildlife biosphere

The Earth's ecosystem is an interconnected web of living organisms and their physical environments. The physical environment includes both living organisms and non-living things, such as rocks, soil, minerals, water and sunlight.

Tip!

Diagonal joins exit from the baseline directly to the next letter. After a diagonal join, the crossbar on the letter t goes above the join.

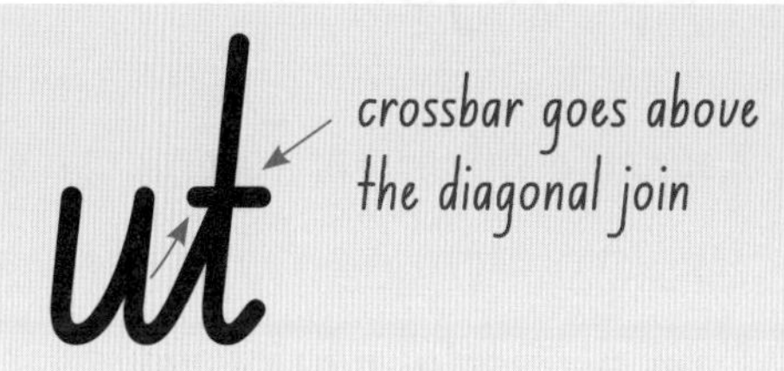


Practise your joins to and from the letter t as you copy the letters and sentences below.

it ut et tu ta at th te nt ti te ct

The ecosystem includes all the different organisms on Earth and their interaction with the physical environment. It includes both living and non-living things, which are connected and interdependent.

How many words can you find in the text above with a diagonal join from e to r? Write them below.

What does it look like where this fish lives? Finish the scene by adding the fish's surroundings.

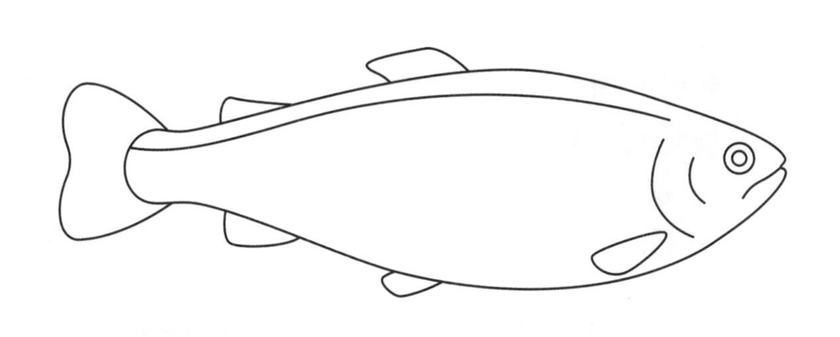

## Drop-in joins

**Learning intention:** To practise drop-in joins

**I am successful when I can:**
- ☐ sit with my back straight
- ☐ hold my pen correctly
- ☐ position my paper
- ☐ drop the letters a, c, d, f, g, o and q into place.

**Tip!** The letters a, c, d, f, g, o and q are dropped into place after a diagonal join.

ea — The dropped-in letter touches the join here.

Practise your drop-in joins as you copy the letters and words below.

ed ec ad ac eq ca if nd ma ic to do ta

land sustain habitat adaptation demand adapt

total population animals bacteria decomposer change

Copy the words below, which relate to the Earth's ecosystem.

| | |
|---|---|
| biosphere ________ | communities ________ |
| biomes ________ | population ________ |
| biodiversity ________ | species ________ |

# Horizontal joins

Learning intention: To practise horizontal joins

**I am successful when I can:**
- ☐ sit with my back straight
- ☐ hold my pen correctly
- ☐ position my paper
- ☐ use horizontal joins for the letters o, r, v, w and x.

slight dip → ou

straight → fa

Practise your horizontal joins as you copy the letters, words and sentence below.

on oq vi fa rg xa od ve ok we oo

of oa wr ol re va oc ra ox ou wi

biomes without various warm survival wind

processes vigorous food organic own consumer cob

The Earth's ecosystem operates as a vigorous and interconnected web,

where energy and nutrients flow through various trophic levels in

food chains and food webs.

**Self-assessment**

Underline your smoothest join. Circle a join that needs more practice.

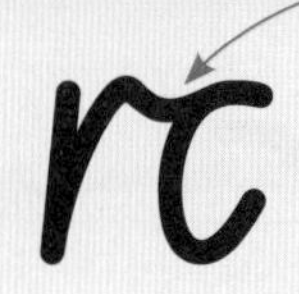

Remember to retrace the top of the letter when completing horizontal joins to anti-clockwise letters.

Practise your horizontal joins as you copy the letters, words and sentence below.

ro va oc wa rc fo od rg og oa

producer warmth forward variety destruction catalogue

Changes or disruptions in one part of the ecosystem can have ripple effects throughout and cause destruction to the species living there.

Choose from the items below and write the correct meaning next to each word.

An event that is interrupted by a problem

Involves using a lot of energy

The part of the Earth where there are living things

A substance that helps living things to grow

| | |
|---|---|
| vigorous | |
| biosphere | |
| nutrient | |
| disruption | |

# Horizontal joins to e

lower dip

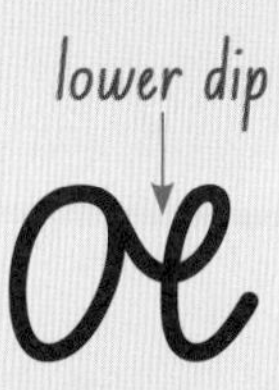

Practise your joins to e as you copy the letters, words and sentences below.

oe re ve we xe oe re ve we xe

reduce vegetation preservation wetland poem renew

A biome is a large ecological area that can be defined by its climate, temperature, geology and vegetation. Biomes have animals and plants that rely on each other. Examples of biomes include deserts, tropical rainforests, tundras, forests and grasslands. A biome can contain many ecosystems.

**Peer feedback**

Ask a partner to review your work and provide feedback on how well you completed your joins.

**Two stars** (two things you did well)

**One wish** (one suggestion on something you can improve)

# Horizontal joins to s

**Learning intention:** To practise horizontal joins to s

**Tip!** You can use a shorter s when joining to s horizontally.

rs

Remember when you join to s diagonally to make the s shorter.

es ts

Practise your joins to s as you copy the letters, words and sentences below.

os rs ts us es is as vs ns ms ds

layers leaves oceans shapes across regions

A variety of biomes exist around the world; each has its own unique characteristics. Tropical rainforests are the most diverse.

**Fine motor skills task:** Follow the steps to sketch the landscape, then colour it in.

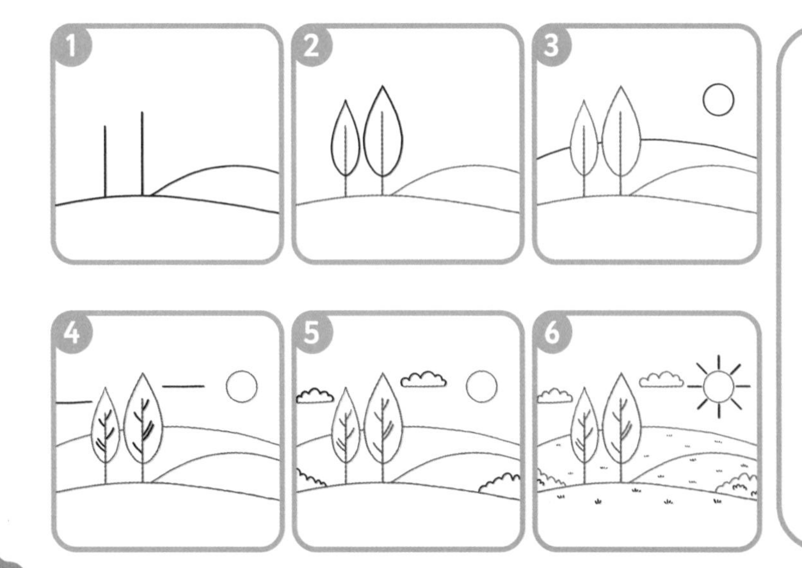

## Consolidating

Copy the passage below.

A habitat is an environment that is the natural home for living things, such as animals and plants, where they can find food, water and shelter. This is where living things interact with each other and the physical environment. Habitats are diverse and are shaped by climate and geography, which affect the reliability of resources.

What kind of habitat do you live in? Can you write three adjectives to describe where you live?

**Teacher feedback**

Practise your keyboarding skills by typing this passage.

# Assessment: Diagonal, drop-in and horizontal joins

Sort these letter pairs into the correct join group.

| | | | | | | | | |
|---|---|---|---|---|---|---|---|---|
| on | ac | ed | aq | in | wn | eg | ve | ib |
| ka | ee | oo | ol | ca | ig | ng | un | ui |
| ea | wi | ni | un | uc | sa | an | wa | it |

Diagonal joins: ____________________

Drop-in joins: ____________________

Horizontal joins: ____________________

Practise your cursive handwriting as you copy the words and sentence below.

regions carbon critical global ocean oxygen science

It is important to protect the Earth's ecosystem by using responsible and sustainable resource management practices that will safeguard it for future generations.

**Self-assessment** Draw a star next to your neatest writing.

Practise your keyboarding skills by typing this passage.

# Revising fluency joins

Remember to slide the base of the letters b, p and s to create smooth fluency joins.

## Fluency joins from b, p and s

**Learning intention:**
To practise fluency joins to make my writing smooth and fluent

bl pe su

Retrace the base of the letter.

Add fluency joins to the letter pairs and words below.

pa se pe pr su bi br sa so se

people bloom preserve sustain soil blueprint protect

Practise your fluency joins from b, p and s as you copy the sentences below.

It is important that people help preserve habitats to maintain the overall health of ecosystems. Adopting sustainable practices can help protect and preserve habitats by allowing plant and animal species to thrive.

**Self-assessment** Draw a star next to your smoothest writing.

Practise your keyboarding skills by typing this passage.

## Word-building task

Practise your fluency joins as you write the different forms of each word below. The first one is done for you.

Remember that we usually drop the e before adding a suffix.

| Base verb | Suffix -ed | Suffix -ing | Noun |
| --- | --- | --- | --- |
| protect | protected | protecting | protection |
| adapt | | | |
| interact | | | |
| conserve | | | |
| interfere | | | |
| reduce | | | |
| preserve | | | |

**Fine motor skills task:** Help Cooper through the jungle maze to find the toucan. Be careful not to touch the edges or lift your pen.

# Fluency joins with double s

**Learning intention:**
To make a double s with the first s the same as the second

**I am successful when I can:**
- ☐ sit with my back straight
- ☐ hold my pen correctly
- ☐ position my paper
- ☐ use fluency joins with double s.

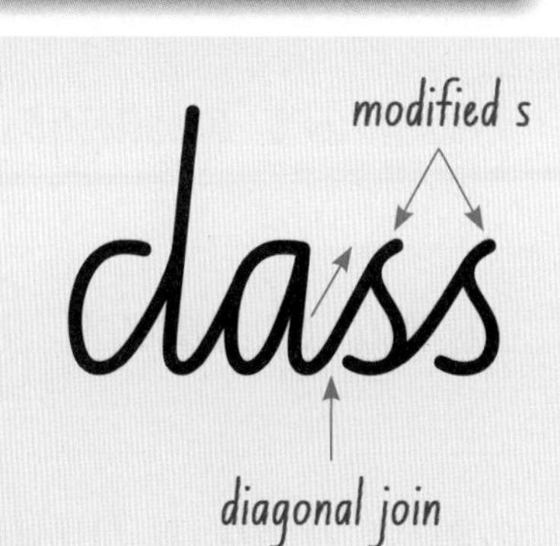

When joining double s using a fluency join, the shape of the second s should match the first. A modified double s is used after diagonal or horizontal joins.

Practise your fluency joins with double s as you copy the words below. Notice that the double s looks different when there is a horizontal join before it.

mossy possible process across gloss toss blossom grass

bliss less asset necessary success discuss essential albatross

Practise your fluency joins with double s as you copy the sentences below.

Successful wildlife habitats require careful management, ensuring that people don't interfere with resources for species. These include shelter, food and water. It is necessary to limit human interaction so that nature can thrive!

**Self-assessment** Draw a star next to your best writing.

Practise your keyboarding skills by typing this passage.

## Practising fluency joins

Practise your fluency joins as you copy the sentences below.

There are a range of different habitats around the world that support a wide variety of species, from the lush rainforests of the Amazon to the arid deserts across inland Australia. All animals and plants adapt to their particular habitat so they can survive. Whether it is the icy Arctic tundra or the vibrancy of the Great Barrier Reef, these environments support life on our planet.

Rewrite these words using fluency joins. Then colour in the rainforest.

| | | | |
|---|---|---|---|
| vibrancy | ______ | supporting | ______ |
| survive | ______ | different | ______ |
| across | ______ | arid | ______ |
| species | ______ | life | ______ |
| variety | ______ | icy | ______ |

# Consolidating

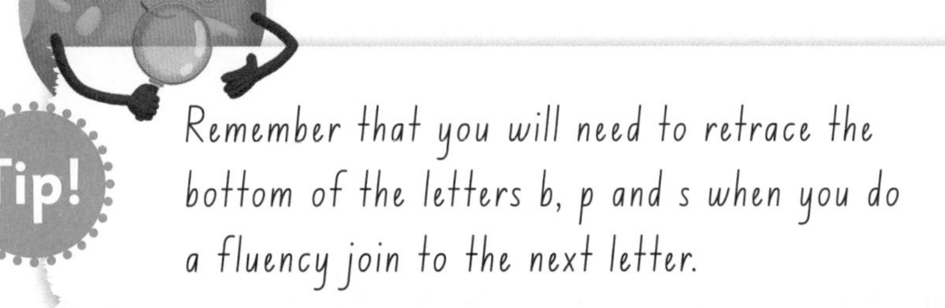


Practise your fluency joins from b, p and s as you copy the sentences below.

Grassland habitats are wide-open spaces containing grasses and smaller plants rather than large trees. There are grassland habitats on most continents, but they have different names. In Africa, they are called savannahs, whereas in North America they are called prairies. Grasslands are in the drier parts of a continent, usually between mountains and deserts, providing a home for diverse plant and animal species.

In the text above, circle all the words that have fluency joins from b, p and s. Write each word below to practise your joins.

# Assessment: Fluency joins

Practise your cursive handwriting and fluency joins as you copy the words below.

scrublands plants between spaces people

supply grasslands sustainable parts blissful

understandable sparse typically burning seasons

From the words above, find the words that have one, two or three fluency joins from b, p and s and list them below.

One fluency join: 

Two fluency joins: 

Three fluency joins: 

Write your own sentence in cursive handwriting. Try to include one word with a double s following a horizontal join and one word with a double s following a diagonal join.

Teacher feedback

# Speed loops and fluency

**Learning intention:**
To use speed loops to make my writing faster and more fluent, focusing on g, j and y

## Speed loops for g, j and y

**I am successful when I can:**

- ☐ sit with my back straight
- ☐ hold my pen correctly
- ☐ position my paper
- ☐ use speed loops for fluency and speed.

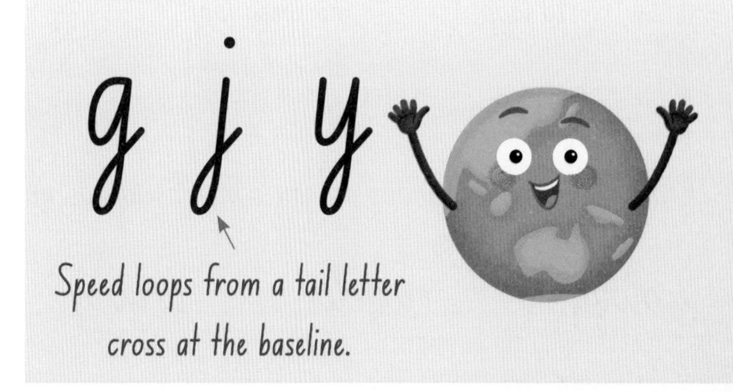

Speed loops from a tail letter cross at the baseline.

Practise your speed loops from g as you copy the letters and words below. (Remember that the letters g, j and y at the end of a word do not need a speed loop.)

ga ga ge ge gi gi go go gr gr gu gu

green growth gorgeous large glacier global grass

germinate region grove garden geology gully encourage

Practise your speed loops from j as you copy the letters and words below.

ja ja ja je je je ji ji ji jo jo jo ju ju ju

journey judging jubilant jungle jacaranda jabiru

Practise your speed loops from y as you copy the letters and words below.

ya ya ye ye yi yi yo yo yr yr yu yu

yacht yield youngest youth yearn skyrail yucca

growing

speed loop no speed loop

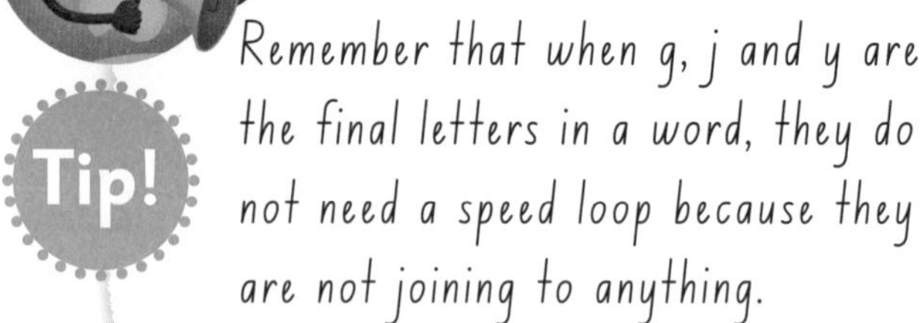

**Tip!** Remember that when g, j and y are the final letters in a word, they do not need a speed loop because they are not joining to anything.

Practise your speed loops as you copy the words and sentences below.

ecology recycle drying gleaming organic juniper

juicy geothermal jagged agriculture mangrove layers

Wildflowers thrive in grasslands across the world, adding colour and attracting pollinators. They include bluebells, wild bergamot and grevilleas.

**Fine motor skills task:** Follow the steps to sketch the flower, then colour it in.

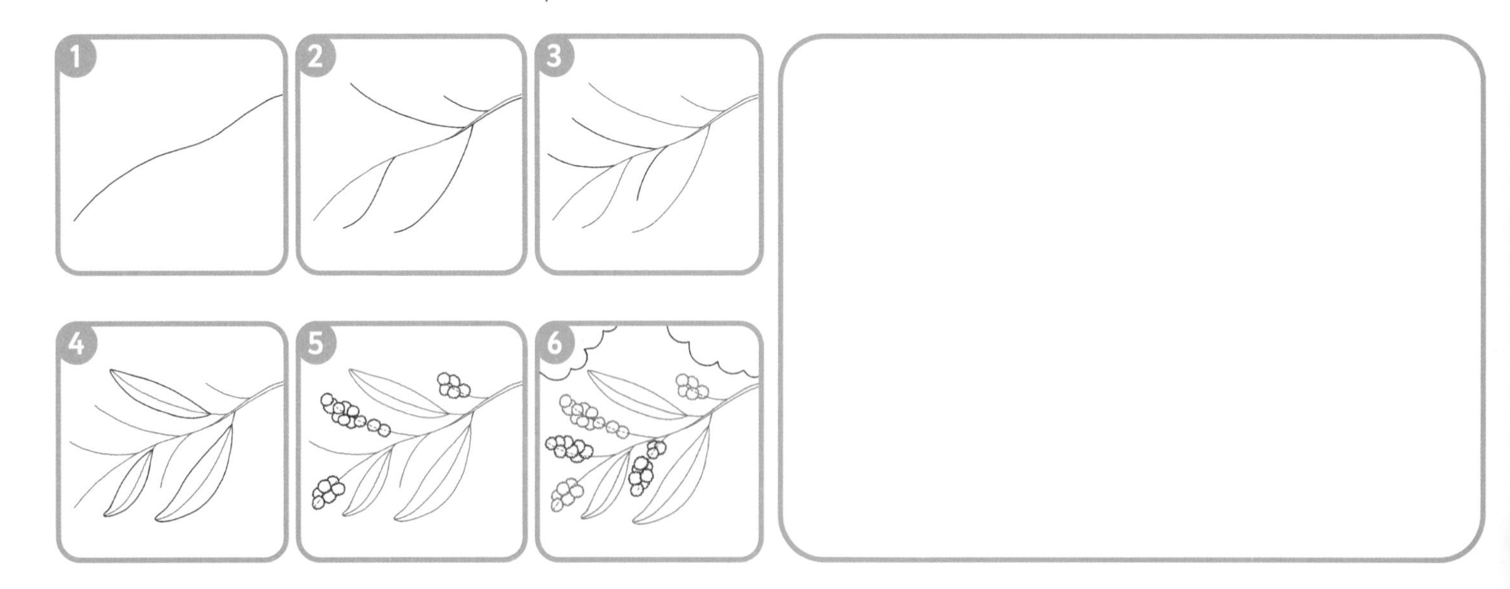

# Speed loops for z

Learning intention:
To use speed loops from the letter z

**I am successful when I can:**

- ☐ sit with my back straight
- ☐ hold my pen correctly
- ☐ position my paper
- ☐ use speed loops when joining from the letter z to increase fluency.

z → z

new z with speed loop

Practise your speed loops for z as you copy the words and sentences below.

za za za ze ze ze zi zi zi zy zy zl zl zz zz

breezy grazing zesty zebras zigzag blaze buzz hazy drizzle

Among the most distinctive animals on the African grasslands are black-

and-white striped zebras. They enjoy grazing on the abundant vegetation.

**Fine motor skills task:** Follow the steps to sketch the zebra.

# Speed loops for f

for coffee cliff

**Tip!** When forming f, use a speed loop to write more quickly.

Practise your speed loops for f as you copy the words and sentences below.

found features flaunt reef colourful fauna

rainfall fish rainforest effect footprint cliff

Coral reefs are found in warm, shallow waters that are rich in biodiversity. They are home to coral colonies, colourful fish and other types of marine life. One of the most famous corals reefs is the Great Barrier Reef, on Australia's north-east coast. It is the largest coral-reef ecosystem in the world and was declared a World Heritage Area in 1981.

**Self-assessment** Circle the words with your best speed loops to f.

Practise your keyboarding skills by typing this passage.

## Practising speed loops

In cursive handwriting, copy these commonly confused words and their definitions.

| | |
|---|---|
| affect (verb) | to produce a change in |
| effect (noun) | a result of something |
| effect (verb) (quite rare) | to make something happen |

Practise your speed loops as you copy the sentences below. Then colour in the seascape.

The warming of ocean waters affects coral reefs, leading to coral bleaching.

The oil spill had an adverse effect on marine life.

The minister tried to effect a change in environmental policy.

# Speed loops for b, h, k and l

Learning intention: To use speed loops for tall letters

I am successful when I can:

- ☐ sit with my back straight
- ☐ hold my pen correctly
- ☐ position my paper
- ☐ use speed loops for forming the letters b, h, k and l.

b h k l

Practise your speed loops as you copy the letters, words and sentences below.

ab eb ak lk ah oh al el ol ul sl cl ch sh wh

research zebu alpine waterfall brisk cobweb elk

peak brink altitudes alpaca elevation herbivores harsh

From snow-capped peaks to alpine valleys, mountain habitats are known for their dramatic landscapes and unique features. These habitats are characterised by their elevation and cold climate. The above photo is of Aoraki (Mt Cook). At 3754 metres, it is New Zealand's highest mountain and a favourite with mountain-climbers.

The letters b, h, k and l do not need a speed loop when they appear at the start of a word.

Practise your speed loops as you copy the sentences below.

Snow leopards are elusive big cats that live in the mountainous regions of Central and South Asia. They have spotted coats that provide excellent camouflage in the rocky, snowy mountain ranges. Snow leopards have adapted to cold climates with their dense fur and furry paws for insulation.

Use coloured pencils to colour in the different shapes in the snow leopard.

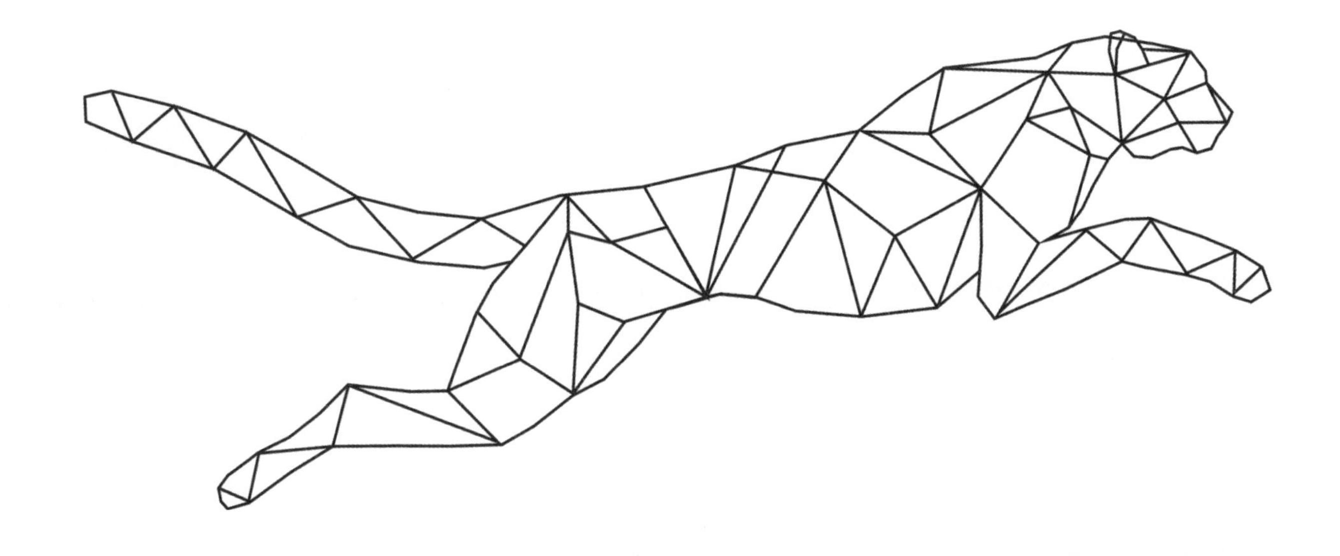

# Fluency and speed

**Learning intention:** To practise fluency and speed

**I am successful when I can:**
- ☐ sit with my back straight
- ☐ hold my pen correctly
- ☐ position my paper
- ☐ use speed loops to increase fluency and speed.

**Tip!** It is important to practise fluency in handwriting so that you can write in an easy and automatic way.

Practise your speed loops as you copy the sentences two or three times. Try to increase your speed as you go.

Alpacas and llamas are native to the Andes Mountains of South America.

Sometimes confused with alpacas, llamas are larger, less woolly and feistier.

Llamas have an elongated face with large, expressive eyes and banana-shaped ears.

Write a sentence to say which animal is your favourite and why you like it.

Practise your speed loops as you copy the words three times. Try to increase your speed in the second and third rows.

blossom branch berry high higher highest

live lively lived bubble kicker skate

Practise your speed loops as you copy the words below.

| | | | |
|---|---|---|---|
| launch | | landmarks | |
| traditions | | harshly | |
| brook | | natural | |
| creek | | landform | |
| sturdy | | skilled | |
| lagoon | | livelihood | |
| breezily | | hillside | |
| effortless | | broken | |
| hollow | | loosely | |
| wetland | | horizon | |
| healthy | | rainforest | |

## Consolidating

Practise your cursive handwriting and speed loops as you copy the sentences below.

Tundra habitats are challenging environments, shaped by extreme climates, and are typically found near the Earth's polar regions. They are very cold places that experience long winters, with temperatures often below freezing. There are fewer species that live in this environment, compared to other ecosystems, due to the extreme conditions.

**Peer feedback**

Ask a partner to review your work and provide feedback on how well you completed your joins.

**Two stars** (two things you did well)

**One wish** (one suggestion on something you can improve)

# Assessment: Speed loops

Practise your speed loops as you copy the poem below. These are the first two verses. You can search for it online if you would like to read the rest of the poem.

"I wandered lonely as a cloud"

by William Wordsworth

I wandered lonely as a cloud
That floats on high o'er vales and hills,
When all at once I saw a crowd,
A host, of golden daffodils;
Beside the lake, beneath the trees,
Fluttering and dancing in the breeze.

Continuous as the stars that shine
And twinkle on the Milky Way,
They stretched in never-ending line
Along the margin of a bay:
Ten thousand saw I at a glance,
Tossing their heads in sprightly dance.

Teacher feedback

# Legibility

## Printing

**Tip!** Print handwriting is often used for labels, maps and different types of forms.

Print each word neatly.

toucan polar bear kangaroo stingray scorpion

crocodile green sea turtle Arctic fox camel

cassowary lion horned lizard zebra panther

From the list above, write the name of one of the animals that lives in these habitats. Print neatly.

| | | | |
|---|---|---|---|
| Arctic tundra | ______ | desert | ______ |
| grassland | ______ | coral reef | ______ |
| rainforest | ______ | wetland | ______ |

**Fine motor skills task:** Follow the steps to sketch the bear, then colour it in.

# Capital letters

Practise your capital letters as you print the names of the continents and oceans on the map.

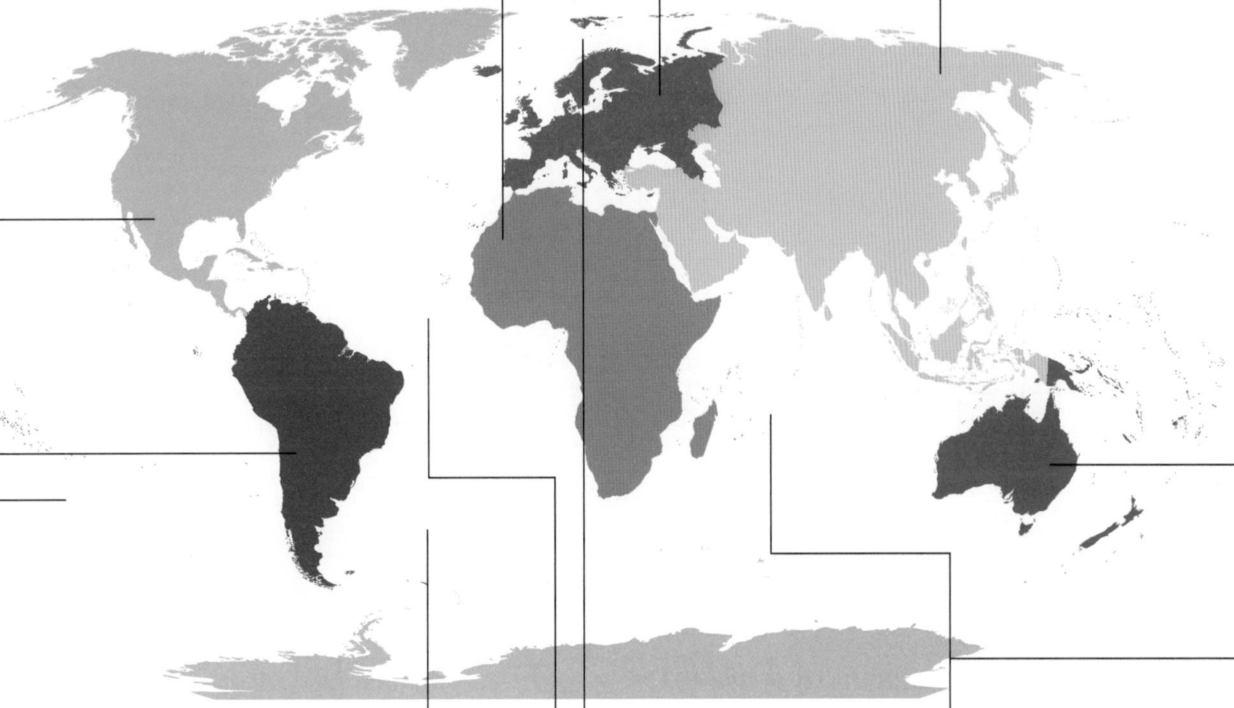

South America

Antarctica

North America

Australia

Africa

Europe

Asia

Southern Ocean

Indian Ocean

Atlantic Ocean

Arctic Ocean

Pacific Ocean

Practise your capital letters as you complete the crossword about animals.

## Across

2 Rainforest animal that moves very slowly (5)
7 Dog-like carnivore of Africa and Asia (5)
8 One of Australia's deadliest reptiles (5, 5)
9 Wool comes from this animal (5)
11 Mammal with long neck (7)
13 Swings through the trees (6)

If you need some hints, your teacher has the answers to the crossword in the Teacher Resource material on Oxford Owl.

## Down

1 Some are free range, and others live caged (8)
3 Biggest mammal on Earth (4, 5)
4 Black jungle cat (7)
5 Big cat with stripes (5)
6 Deadly desert arachnid (8)
8 Colourful insect (9)
10 Considered the king of the jungle (4)
12 Common farm animal (3)

# Spacing

Why is it important to practise spacing in handwriting?

Spacing is important because it helps to make your writing easier to read. Even letter spacing makes your writing more legible.

Tick the sentence that is most evenly spaced.

Writing  that is  evenly spaced  is easier  to read. ☐
Writing that is evenly spaced is easier to read. ☐
Writing that is  evenly  spaced is easier  to read. ☐

Copy the sentence below twice and try to develop an even spacing between letters.

Rainforests are some of the most intricate ecosystems on Earth.

Copy the sentences below, then use a highlighter pen to highlight the line with the best word spacing.

Rainforests are lush habitats found in tropical regions near the equator.

They are characterised by lots of rainfall and year-round warmth,

creating excellent conditions for a wide variety of plants and animals.

# Size

tropical tropical

even letter size uneven letter size

Tip! Keeping your letters an even size is an important skill to master. It will help increase your fluency.

Practise consistent letter size and spacing as you copy the sentences below.

There are two types of rainforest: tropical and temperate. They have distinct features that make them unique to their location and climate. Temperate rainforests are cooler than tropical rainforests. A temperate rainforest in Australia is Barrington Tops National Park in New South Wales. Tropical rainforests are found closer to the equator and in countries across South and Central America, Africa and South-East Asia. A famous Australian tropical rainforest is the Daintree in Queensland.

**Self-assessment** Draw a star next to the line with the most consistent letter size.

Practise your keyboarding skills by typing this passage.

# Slope

**Tip!**

Having a consistent slope to your writing will help with legibility. Use the slope card at the back of the book to guide you. Place it behind the page you are writing on to help keep the slope of your writing consistent.

Write this word five times, using the slope lines as a guide.

equator

Circle the words with an inconsistent slope. Then, write all of the words using a consistent slope.

temperate warm emergent coasts

canopy dense rainfall climate

Practise a consistent slope as you copy the sentences below.

The hallmark of a rainforest is its towering trees, which form a multi-layered canopy.

Tropical rainforests are home to numerous species of animals and plants.

Although temperate rainforests have fewer plant and animal species, they are home to many birds, amphibians, insects, reptiles and large mammals.

# Labelling

The layers of a tropical rainforest are shown below. Next to each heading, add dot points describing each layer. You may want to do some online research before you begin. The first one is done for you. Print neatly.

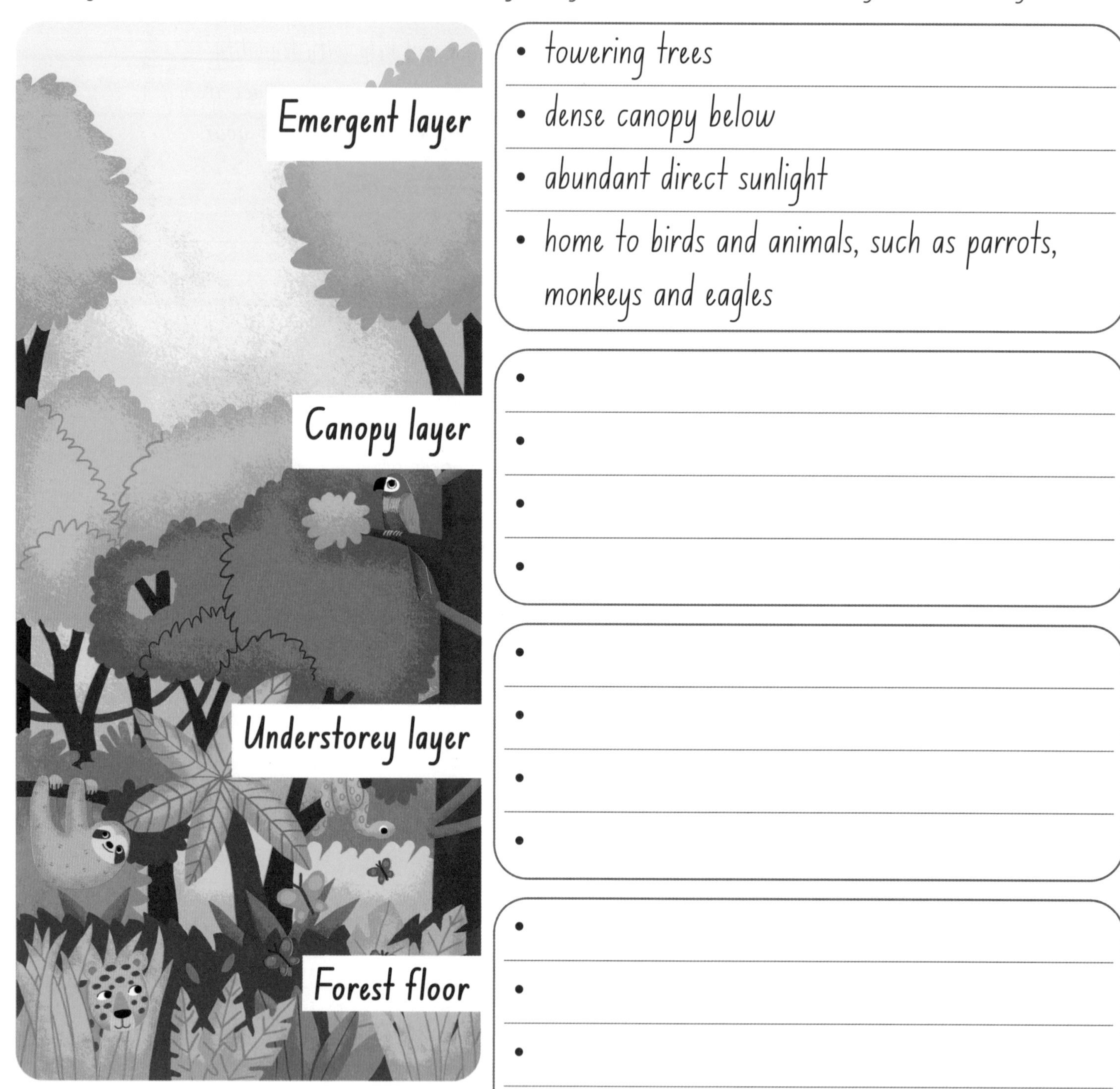


**Emergent layer**
- towering trees
- dense canopy below
- abundant direct sunlight
- home to birds and animals, such as parrots, monkeys and eagles

**Canopy layer**
-
-
-
-

**Understorey layer**
-
-
-
-

**Forest floor**
-
-
-
-

Using your dot points, write a descriptive sentence about a rainforest in cursive handwriting.

# Practising size, spacing and slope

**Learning intention:**
To practise maintaining consistent size, spacing and slope in handwriting

**I am successful when I can:**
☐ keep my letter size, spacing and slope even.

Practise your speed loops as you copy the sentences below.

A unique feature of a rainforest is its

towering trees, which form the canopy.

These trees can reach staggering heights,

with emergent trees piercing through the

canopy to receive maximum sunlight.

The canopy itself creates a dense and

shaded environment beneath it.

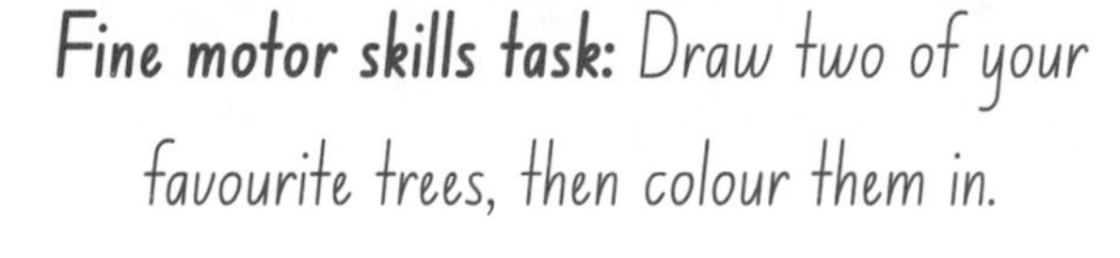

**Fine motor skills task:** Draw two of your favourite trees, then colour them in.

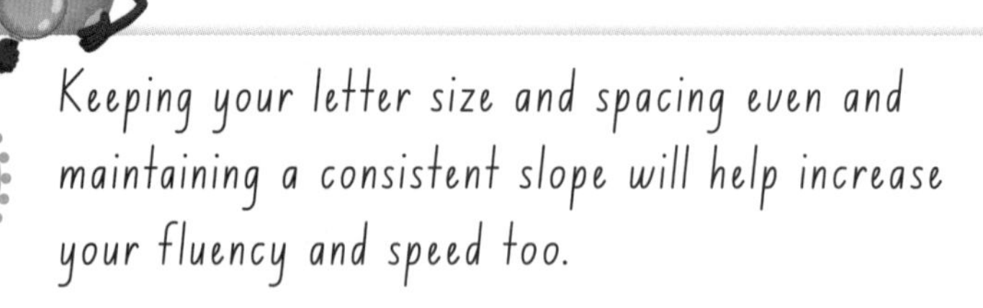


Practise your cursive handwriting as you copy the sentences below.

Rainforests are home to a multitude of animals and plants. Rainforests support a web of interconnected species, each playing a role in the balance and functioning of this intricate ecosystem. Some species that live in rainforests include monkeys, sloths, orangutans, gorillas, frogs and chameleons.

Finish the scene by adding the chameleon's surroundings in a rainforest.

# Fluency

These words are often misspelt. Practise your cursive handwriting and speed loops as you copy them.

calendar fulfil separate maintenance quiet

beautiful experience receive privilege Arctic

achieve accommodate fascinating definitely foreign

## Word-building task

In cursive handwriting, add the morphographs (word parts) together. The first one is done for you.

**Tip!** Remember to change the y to an i before adding the suffix. We usually drop the e before adding a suffix.

create + ive = creative

peace + ful + ly = ______

pro + port + ion = ______

un + ex + plain + ed = ______

re + late + ion = ______

noise + y + ness = ______

un + like + ly + ness = ______

re + cent + ly = ______

in + cure + able = ______

city + es = ______

room + y + ness = ______

The rainforest is home to some fascinating and unique birds. Practise your speed, fluency and cursive handwriting as you copy the sentences on this page and the next.

## Cassowary

Cassowaries are large, flightless birds that are native to the rainforests of

north-eastern Australia and New Guinea. They have striking blue facial skin and

a helmet-like casque on their heads. The casque protects the cassowary as it moves

through dense forest. Cassowaries have three-toed feet with a sharp claw on the

inner toe that helps them dig for food and ward off predators.

## Scarlet macaw

An iconic bird that is native to the rainforests of Central and South America is the scarlet macaw. Known for its vibrant colours, it spends much of its time in the canopy. Scarlet macaws are beautiful, large parrots and can measure up to 83 cm from beak to tail.

## Toucan

Found in the rainforests of Central and South America, toucans have an unusual appearance. Their most distinctive feature is their large and colourful bill.

Copy the sentence below. Then use a highlighter pen to highlight the adverbs.

Vividly coloured toucans soar gracefully through the dense rainforest canopy.

Copy this definition of an adverb.

An adverb is a word that modifies or describes a verb, adjective or another adverb.

Copy these adverbs.

kindly carefully warmly safely

beautifully politely bravely gracefully

honestly vividly quickly always

certainly softly foolishly usually

In cursive handwriting, write about a bird of the rainforest and describe its behaviour. Include at least three adverbs and use complete sentences.

## Consolidating

Practise your speed and fluency as you copy the sentences below.

Animals and plants have adapted to survive in their environment over many years. This has helped them to improve their chances of survival. An "adaptation" is a feature of a living thing that helps it adjust to its habitat. For example, chameleons are able to change colour. They do this to blend in with their surroundings, regulate their body temperature or attract a potential mate. Koalas have adapted to eat only eucalyptus leaves. This gives them an advantage because the leaves are toxic to most animals.

**Fine motor skills task:** Follow the steps to sketch the bird, then colour it in.

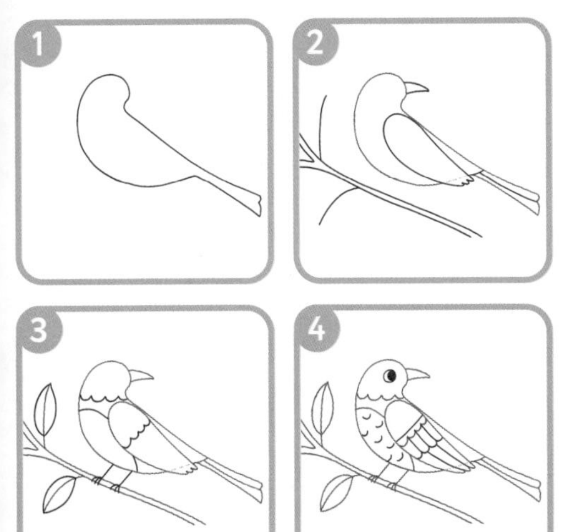

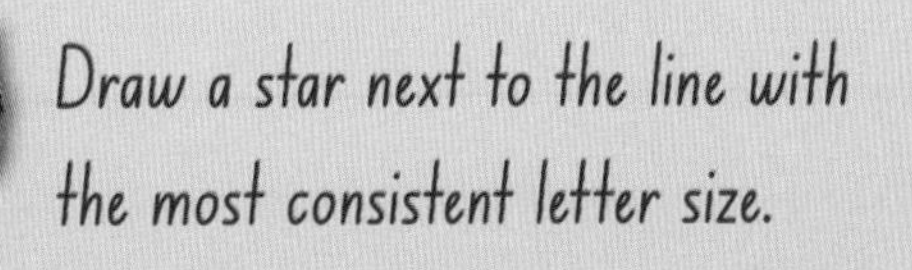

**Self-assessment**

Draw a star next to the line with the most consistent letter size.

Practise your keyboarding skills by typing this passage.

# Speed test

It is important to master fluent and speedy handwriting. Practising your speed in forming letters and words can help to improve overall proficiency.

Read the sentence and try to remember it. Write out the sentence as many times as you can within two minutes using fluency joins and speed loops.

Animals can be classified into different groups: mammals, birds, reptiles, amphibians, invertebrates and fish.

**Self-assessment**

Rate your fluency   

Rate your legibility   

# Developing a style

Tip!

Handwriting can be adjusted to suit the purpose. When you are taking notes, you might use speed loops to ensure your writing is quick. For labelling maps or filling out forms, you would use print handwriting. If you are creating a presentation or a document for a special occasion, you might add more flourishes to your handwriting.

Trace and then copy the flourished letters below.

a b c d e f g h i j k l m

n o p q r s t u v w x y z

A B C D E F G H I J K L M

N O P Q R S T U V W X Y Z

Write your name and school address using flourished lettering, and then sign off with your personal signature.

Signature: ______________________

# Note-taking

Note-taking is an important skill to learn. Taking notes helps to keep a record of information that you have read or listened to. Sometimes, note-taking may not be very neat, but it should still be legible.

Complete some research on an animal you would like to learn more about. Find out about its appearance, diet, habitat and behaviour.

1. Use the listed websites below to help you research.
2. Write your notes in the box below.

Tip! Use speed loops to help you write notes quickly.

Your note-taking should include the following information.

- An introduction
- Appearance – what does your animal look like?
- Diet – what does it eat?
- Habitat – where does it live?
- Behaviour – how does it move and behave?

Useful sources of information

- Your school library
- https://kids.nationalgeographic.com/animals
- https://animalfactguide.com
- https://www.softschools.com/facts/animals

# Consolidating

Start with a compelling introduction that provides a brief overview of your chosen animal and why it's interesting or important. Use your best cursive handwriting, ensuring that your work is neat and legible.

## Writing activity

Use your research and your notes to write an engaging and informative text about your chosen animal.

Draw your chosen animal.

Practise your keyboarding skills by typing your text.

# Assessment: Legibility

*Practise your speed loops and cursive handwriting as you copy the sentences below.*

Many species around the world are facing the threat of extinction due to habitat loss, climate change and other human-related factors. Rainforest species are under enormous threat, mainly due to habitat loss and illegal poaching. Some of the endangered species found in rainforests include orangutans, pygmy elephants, leopards and gorillas. Conservation efforts are crucial to protect these species and preserve the delicate balance of rainforest ecosystems.

**Teacher feedback**